Love Medicine and One Song

Sâkihtowin-Maskihkiy Êkwa Pêyak-Nikamowin

GREG SCOFIELD

LOVE MEDICINE

and

ONE SONG

SÂKIHTOWIN-MASKIHKIY ÊKWA PÊYAK-NIKAMOWIN

GREGORY SCOFIELD

POLESTAR
BOOK PUBLISHERS

Polestar Book Publishers acknowledges the support of the Canada Council,
the British Columbia Ministry of Small Business, Tourism and Culture, and
the Department of Canadian Heritage – Multiculturalism Program and
Book Publishing Industry Development Program.

Cover artwork and design by Jim Brennan
Author photograph by Kelli Speirs
Printed in Canada

CANADIAN CATALOGUING IN PUBLICATION DATA
Scofield, Gregory, 1966-
        Love medicine and one song
ISBN 1-896095-27-5
Poems in English and Cree.
1. Love poetry, Canadian (English)*   2. Love poetry, Canadian (Cree)*
3. Erotic poetry, Canadian (English)*
4. Erotic poetry, Canadian (Cree)*   I. Title.
PS8587.C614L6 1997   C811'.54   C97-910114-X
PR9199.3.S297L6 1997

LIBRARY OF CONGRESS CARD CATALOG NUMBER: 95-65825

in Canada
Polestar Book Publishers
P.O. Box 5238, Station B
Victoria, British Columbia
Canada   V8R 6N4
http://mypage.direct.ca/p/polestar/

in the United States
Polestar Book Publishers
P.O. Box 468
Custer, WA
USA   98240-0468

5   4   3   2   1

For Kim and Dean, my inspiration.
And for all who thought it impossible.

Sâkihtowin-Maskihkiy Êkwa Pêyak-Nikamowin
Love Medicine and One Song

love, desire, pleasure

tension

Twelve Moons and the Dream

lovers are broken up

Love Medicine and One Song

how to get him back?
love medicine?

TANSI NITOTEMAK!

AYA, KOTAK MÎNA NIWÎ-ÂTOTÊN,
SÂKIHAN Ê-WÎ-ACÎMAK.

I remember hearing old-time stories about love medicine. It is said that under its powerful spell one becomes completely obsessed, inexplicably determined to be near the person who cast it.

I have always been warned about such medicine. "Pêyahtihk," the old people would say. "It is not to be taken lightly for the consequences are great and, if used improperly, often fatal."

One such story was told to me by my late auntie, Georgina (Houle) Young. It is about an older woman who was called Ôhowkôt, who worked medicine on a young man with whom she was taken, but she had been unsuccessful in catching his attention.

Now, Ôhowkôt's medicine was strong for she had gone to see a well-known medicine man whose expertise in matters of love was of reknown throughout the land.

Sure enough, as promised by the medicine man, the young man fell deeply in love with Ôhowkôt. They were married and they moved up north, far away from family and friends.

However, over the years Ôhowkôt grew bored of the man's child-like ways, and she became restless to find a man with whom she could feel equal. She began to stay away for days at a time and it was rumoured that she had found another lover.

But still the young man remained fiercely loyal, refusing to believe his wife's infidelity while professing his love for her wherever he went. He carried on as usual, working the whole day through to come home at night to an empty house, a house which he kept neat and tidy.

One night there was a knock upon the door.

"Forgive me," said a strange man, "but there has been a terrible accident. I am sorry to tell you your wife is dead."

"Ha!" laughed the young man. "You must be mistaken. My wife is visiting her family."

"Perhaps," replied the stranger, "it is you who are mistaken. She has been with her lover only a few miles from here. Last night his house caught fire and both of them are dead."

But as the weeks turned into months the young man still did not believe the story. He went out of his mind searching the towns and woods, near and far. He took to keeping vigil at the window each and every night. He even went back to their old home, looking for her. But as with the times before, no one had seen or heard from her.

And so, over the years the young man grew sicker and sicker. Finally, when he was on his deathbed a healer was summoned. First the old man shook his rattle over him and then placed two small white stones on his eyes.

Sure enough, after a while the stones turned black and the old man exclaimed, "Haw! I've found the sickness. It is love sickness."

But it was too late. The young man died that very same night.

"This is a terrible thing," said the old man. "The medicine is far too strong. Ôhowkôt maci-manitow! She is greedy even from the world beyond."

Today, such stories carry as much power as they did long ago. Among many First Nations people, love and the old-time medicines are very much a part of our spiritual reality and existence. Though they are seldom known or heard of in non-First Nations circles, they continue to be practiced or used by those who possess knowledge. Importantly, as with all things pertaining to the spirit or spirit world, we are taught to honour these gifts which come from Kisê-manitow, the Creator.

Therefore our elders, our teachers, impart upon us — the students and eventual grannies and grandpas — the greatest responsibilities: truth, integrity and, above all, respect. It is perhaps for this reason that our sacred ceremonies and healing medicines have not been made public.

As for me, I am still very young and have much to learn. These poems or medicine-songs are mine and come from a sacred place within. I have made tobacco offerings to ask for the help and guidance of The Grandmothers and Grandfathers, and to honour my Two Spirits as well as my two loves, to whom this book is dedicated. In doing so, I have asked permission to share them with you, to present them in the most honourable, honest and sacred way I know: to sing my experience of love in both of my languages, Cree and English. It is with respect and love I offer to you, *Sâkihtowin-Maskihkiy Êkwa Pêyak-Nikamowin.*

I am truly grateful to the many people who have supported me during the evolution of this project:

The British Columbia Arts Council provided the necessary financial support.

Love and thanks to my friend and publisher, Michelle Benjamin, who believed in this project from the first day, whose enthusiasm echoes in each and every poem and whose knowledge and expertise I've come to trust implicitly.

As well, my sincere gratitude goes to Emiko Morita, Katy Moore and Margaret Devenny from Polestar, for their praise, laughter and continued confidence.

I would also like to thank my sister and friend, mother and mentor, Maria Campbell, whose insight, support and advice has been of primary importance. Maria, kî-sâkihtan!

I am also greatly indebted to such fine writers as Larissa Lai, Joanne Arnott, Patrick Lane, Marilyn Dumont and many others for their continued support, their depth of insight, and willingness to confront difficult issues.

And, of course, love and respect to Louise Halfe (Sky-Dancer) for walking the road with me. Louise, kî-sâkihtan!

Also, thanks to my life-long friends who are very much family: Kelli Speirs, Melanie Speirs, Carol Kellman, Candace Gordon and Linda King. I hope they know how often their love and support has propelled me forward.

Ever so importantly, my love and gratitude to my partner and friend, Kim Pedersen, who never ceases to amaze me, whose unconditional love has given life to this very book. In particular, I am grateful for her patience, her support and willingness to share my love. Kim, kî-sâkihtan!

My late mother and friend, Dorothy Scofield, not only taught me to be strong but, from some unseen world, continues to support and guide me through each and every difficult phase. Mom, kî-sâkihtan!

Also importantly, my late auntie, Georgina (Houle) Young, whose life-long gift of love, laughter, language and stories are a constant well from which I draw strength and pride. Auntie, kî-sâkihtan!

Finally, to Dean, the source of shadows and songs, my deepest respect and prayers, wherever you may be. Dean, kî-sâkihtan!

To the reader, I hope that you will know and

find here the most healing of all medicines –
love! Use it carefully and truthfully. Be it yours,
always!

In friendship.
All My Relations,
Scof
March 1997
Maple Ridge, B.C.

Tansi Nitotemak: Greetings to my relations
Aya, kotak mîna niwî-âtotên, sâkihan ê-wî-acîmak:
Well, I will also tell another story, I am going to tell about
    love
Pêyahtihk: to walk softly, to give something great thought
    or consideration
Ôhowkôt: Owl-nose
maci-manitow: the devil
Ôhowkôt maci-manitow: Owl-nose is a devil
Kisê-manitow: the Creator
kî-sâkihtan: I love you

Today in the afternoon love passed
Over his perfect flesh, and on his lips.
Over his flesh, which is the mould
Of beauty, passed love's fever,
  Uncontrolled
By any ridiculous shame of the form
  Of the enjoyment...

From He Came To Read,
C.P. Cavafy (1863–1933)

EARTH AND TEXTURES

❧ Earth and Textures
for Kim

îh, îh
she is the earth lodge
opening her arms,
softly calling,
pî-pîhtâkwey, pî-pîhtâkwey.

îh, îh
she is pîhtwawikamik
where I come
to cry the dry stone
from my throat.

îh, îh
she is earth medicine ties
hanging from trees,
a sacred moon mother
birthing stars
for my dream path.

pehtâw, pehtâw
she is the song
of frogs and crickets
tickling my feet
so always I am rooted.

îh, îh: look, look
pî-pîhtâkwey, pî-pîhtâkwey: come in, come in
pîhtwawikamik: the sacred lodge where the pipe is smoked
pehtâw, pehtâw: listen, listen (as in to hear very closely)

❧He Is

earthworm, caterpillar
parting my lips, he is

slug slipping between my teeth
and down, beating

moth wings, a flutter
inside my mouth

he is snail kissing dew
from the shell of my ears,

spider crawling breath tracks
down my neck and weaving

watersnake, he is
swamp frog croaking my chest

hopping from nipple to nipple,
he is mouse

on my belly running circles
and circles, he is

grouse building his nest
from marsh grass and scent,

weasel digging eggs
between my legs,

he is hungry, so hungry
turtle, he is

slow, so slow
nuzzling and nipping

I crack
beneath the weight of him,

he is mountain lion
chewing bones, tasting marrow

rain water
trickling down my spine,

he is spring bear
ample and lean

his berry tongue quick,
sweet from the feasting.

☙Ôchîm ✦ His Kiss

his mouth brushing mine
is a flat stone
skipping the lake's surface
and oh his tongue
a spawning fish jumps
over and over the waterfall
is maskwa pawing
all his winter hunger
so I yield up roots and berries
and lie back
my whole abundant self
curling fingers in his hair
while he nudges and strokes
the earth of me weightless
firefly in his ear
humming and buzzing higher and
higher yes yes yes
beating his rhythms
through my body,
a low water moon drum
till my mouth is dry of song.

maskwa: bear

🍃 Waking

Early morning fluttering above our bed
moth of light

kissing his chest
rises and falls

in slow lava motion.
The mouth's wonder begins

where flesh is cut deepest,
where sleep's damp tongue

has left its humid pool
and gathered scent.

His legs are heavy oaks
having fallen in the night.

Now he's wide open and breathing
his long lazy dreams

as one knows rain
by the wind's fragrant song

and when his arm
throws back the day, he stretches

the sun to fullness. Flies swarm
from the black matted grass

and heat. He is muskeg.
I am muskeg.

This room, our bed a swamp
we swim in

our own damp, translucent pool
stunned as any fish
caught dreaming.

Morning in the White Room

In the white room
we had joined
the way two rivers meet;
swollen from days
of endless rain, overflowing
our opposite banks which met
here, in the middle
flooding the floor
with our lips and limbs
like so many gasping fish.

We had made it
our celebration, a holy gathering
of the empty walls
and all that haunts them.
Take for instance,
your aqueous silhouette,
how it danced
to my mouth's sacred song.
And our bodies,
painted black and clinging
to invisible horses
galloped across the walls,
overtook the room like warriors
whooping our victory.

And in the morning
when the sun spoke up,
scolded clean the walls
we laughed like children,
shy in our nakedness,
scheming like raven
the last meddling rays.

◣ Five Images

Under his arms, my mouth's
buzzing firefly
hovers and lands
the wet swamp grass
heavy with dew, releasing
the muskeg's secret scent
so he bends, breaks
beneath tongue tracks,
so the ducks
fly up

circle his nipples, pink/
purple as the summer lilies
afloat
with tiny-eared frogs
straining to hear
my moon's midnight song

sweeping
the small of his back,
chasing shadows from the dip
where insects doze,
lazy from the heat,
dreaming their wings to spread,
to lift them
into flight

like his mouth poised
and opening,
crawling water beetle into mine
and sliding me down

to where the bullrushes
leap and dance,
to where
all springs to life

and the rocks
speak without words.

Hunger

This is the mouth's madness.
This is my tongue, my plaything
collecting dew,
drinking with all its senses;
air spiced with rain
and you, unbathed,
sweet swamp, muskeg in June.

This is the tongue's madness.
This is the ruby
in all its precious forms.
It moves
on the wet floor in the Amazon.
A slow, lazy species,
shy as gecko.
Not meaning elusive but hypnotic,
and charming
a basket of cobras.

This is the night's madness
and the mouth's great sorrow.
This is the hour
I drift up and out of bed,
all of its space
whirling in my eyes
as the moon floats teasingly by,
she, looking rather full.

Unread Letter, November 24th

Here, the days pass into night
silently grey, relentless
as the fluid clouds
overtaking the sky, overflowing
the ditches
like last month's leaves.

Moon has been a stranger,
a sliver on Tuesday
but somewhere ever since.
Not even the dogs
bark at night, and the cat
seldom leaves her basket.

Last night,
damp to the bone
I struck a fire,
stretched out on the floor
composing all I'd say
should the rain suddenly stop
and sparrow come
chirping you the song –

chirping as he did
last July
when I cast your name
like a wishing stone.

Now it seems
a hundred years ago.
I had the flesh of new leaves,
the smell of moss
and all that grows wild.

Still, you are welcome,
welcome as the sun
should it ever shine.

❧ More Rainberries (The Hand Game)

The softest, deepest warmth
between his shoulders
is where my lips
take momentary rest, where
breathing becomes ritual
transcends into ceremony

pushing the song up and out
of his skin
so lowly he sings
rainberries form and glisten,
finding my tongue

each mole, every fine hair
speaking the soul's language,
tossing up
the body's ancient rhythm
like hand game bones,
painted sticks marking
the secret centres, where

my hands, delirious with song
sway to his drumming,
rock to each beat swooping
down, down
to the muskeg, where

scented rainberries
fat as frogs
explode in my mouth,

his deepest warmth

a sweet taste
painting my lips.

No Language

What is it he pulls to the surface,
a tribe of fish
flapping their tails
in my blood's lake?
What is it he calls to my lips,
little redbird
humming in mid-flight?
What is it he sweeps
ivory and pale blue,
a laughing cloud
breaking the rock of me?
What is it he leaves
in the marrow,
a circle-backed snail
worming through my bones,
trailing his silk thread
down to my toes?

What is it he speaks,
old earth and roots
moving across his tongue
and mine?

Always, it crumbles
in my mouth
before discovery.

❧ Offerings

I lie over him
a sacred mountain
where black bear
paws the earth, sniffs
for songs

I move over him
like prairie wind,
my hands
scented summer rain,
the storm a distant rumbling

I glide over hills
float through valleys,
my tongue
kissed by moon,
my mouth
the ancient canyon
where wild horses
gallop the sky

I drink from moonlit pools,
sing with frogs
so always
sweet water
runs from my mouth
and becomes poetry

MY DRUM, HIS HANDS

ꙮ My Drum, His Hands

over the bones, over the bones
stretched taut
my skin, the drum

softly he pounds   tension
humming

as black birds dance,
their feathers
gliding over lips, they drink
the stars
from my eyes
depart like sun
making way for moon
to sing, to sing
my sleeping

my sleeping song
the sky bundle

he carries me to dreams,
his hands wet
and gleaming

my drum aching

❧ His Flute, My Ears

piyis êkwa ê-tipiskâk êkwa
ôh, êkwa kâ-kimiwahk,
kâ-kimiwahk

earth smells, love medicine
seeping into my bones
and I knew
his wind voice
catching
the sleeping leaves

ôh, êkwa kâ-kimiwahk,
kâ-kimiwahk

I dreamed
him weaving spider threads
into my hair,
fingers of firefly
buzzing ears, the song
his flute
stealing clouds from my eyes

kâ-kimiwahk
I woke

numb in my bones.

piyis êkwa ê-tipiskâk êkwa
ôh, êkwa kâ-kimiwahk,
kâ-kimiwahk
At last it was night
oh, and it rained,
it rained

≷ Offering: 1996

This long drought
scorches the skin,
blisters me in places

most vulnerable; inner thighs,
tailbone, nape of neck —
the sacred temples.

Since your body eclipsed
I've swallowed the moon,
pretended light from others

and my bones did crack
and from my mouth
grew many unhappy weeds.

Where once were drums
and flutes and songs
there is silence,

incurable as the heart, hopeless
like your resurrection
I breathe all my breath

to conjure
what I hold most sacred:

your full, coaxing mouth,
the two perfect moles
I've named and kissed
the back of your legs,

that smooth dip
between your cheeks, the musk
from the shell of your arms

which left underwater
is a potion, a drug
lulling me to dizziness,

lifting me upward
like sage and cedar
singing to the heavens, singing

to guide you home.

❧ Unhinged

Sure
I've imagined you,
my unkempt soldier
alone in your room
pulling up all your heated secrets,
coming unglued
like the dovetail joints
of my antique dresser.

You are exquisite at this hour,
pure milkweed,
opalescent as the moon
turning down her blind eye.
And always, dangerous.

Sure
I've slipped the curve
of your backside, slipped between
your thighs,
my seasoned lips mouthing
the peach song
beneath your scrotum.
So, sing my breather, play me
the whole black night.
Sing me, anoint me
with your musk, ear wax,
your navel dew.

Sure
I've imagined you
alone in your room,
alone with me
in a phone booth, a theatre,
the back seat of a bus
travelling somewhere so solitary
the landscape has no memory.

Sure, my unkempt soldier
I've dreamed you unhinged
and raging,
your seed exploding like a bullet,
my death
merely a fading pulse.

🦢 You, the Voyeur

And the very thought stirs me,
your private body not so private,
that monument of flesh and bone,
its hardness concealed
though once I saw it, caught it
briefly peeking your desire,
singing its prisoner's song
through the bars of your bones.

Because of this
the thought of you
free and stretching
brings such wet to my mouth,
a wet so brilliant
it far surpasses the law
determining
which way flows the sea.

And so, it stands to reason
in the depth of your eyes
my mouth is the sea
I have laid upon your chest,
sweetly sucked the fish
from their pools,
crushed my waves against clavicle,
receded this tongue into caverns
you only imagined.

So many nights have passed
over me
like fingers heavy with rain.
Always
you are there, a breath
without contemplation or confusion.
And always,
I am greedy to swallow the moon –

and you,
watching from some secret place.

For My Love,
Appealing to His Obstinate Skin

Really, you are shamelessly cruel
to be such a persistent ghost.
One day
I will cease to be the word acrobat
swinging from café to café,
drunk on coffee and you
and all these hazardous nights
cherubs flying from my mouth
for the world to see
wobbling on the table
their fat legs,
their delicate wings fumbling
to make you
a poem.

One day
I will spit in the face
of the censored moon,
so dull and incurably grey
like all her lovers
yet, she has the clouds
to move over her,
sing in her ear the way I've sung
for you.
Really, it's all so tedious.

Imagine a lake of want
trapped beneath your fingertips.
Imagine
how your hands would swell,
hang like rocks, useless.
It's tortuous, even barbaric
speaking aloud your obstinate skin,
though in doing so,
one must consider your loveliness,
those narcotic lips
crying out like gulls in the bay.

Really, you are the cruellest
of any silences —
the night is your hair,
the rain, your lips, and oh
damn the stars,
those two most angelic moles.

Long Ride Home

The crevice of you, that gorge
between hip and thigh,

that smooth divide, flat-out
as any highway

a long ride home. Green light
my red-night traveller, I'll ride

the map
as far as it goes, drive you

the way you were meant
to be driven: hard to the touch,

light on the brakes – Go on
my explorer, stretch all your miles

stretch me to last, stretch me
your long brown legs

switch on the cruise, boy
sing me to navel valley,

sing me down to peachland,
I'm humming like hot concrete

beneath the skin, bed me down
you awesome flier, lift me

to a higher altitude — Go on
take the wheel, take it

and cruise me
a slow moon mile.

⬎ Drive By

For months now
the little house has sat empty,
half buried in seasons
and grass
your parents return to cut
once in a blue,

blue moon
though you, the belligerent ghost
never come.
I hang on their moons
birthing you poems
like some love-sick fool.

For months now
I've been out of dark streets
and unbound thoughts.
For months now
I've crept by, headlights blaring
all my jagged dreams,
these shameless nights
and moon's snicker.

Yes, I could sit in the driveway
wait an eternity
if it meant
one night's rest.

For months now, just once
I was hoping
to see you at the window.
No miracle. No fuss.
Just you, as before
and the whole endless night,
the TV glare
allowing one passing

glimpse.

I've Looked For You

in the blackest night, calling
at the edge of a cliff
knowing, should you answer,
I'd grow wings.

I've looked for you

in the likeliest of places:
prairie cafés, washrooms in Arizona,
airports connecting countries
and lovers and

I've seen you, tall as a cedar,
reaching to the heavens,
wings of raven on top
trimmed short, neat and convincing

my hopeful eyes
till you felt their burning
and turned around.
I've searched for you

breathless and parched
as the gauzy summer,
drank your name
from water fountains

and remained thirsty. I've pressed
my face to the very moon,
cursed the stars from the sky
knowing as I do

the dark is to blame,
how big the world really is
and chances are small, fleeting
with each passing day

and yet, I am here
falling from so many edges
even the rocks below
know your silence.

TWELVE MOONS AND THE DREAM

for Michelle

❧ Niski-pîsim

MARCH ✦ THE GOOSE MOON

Reconcile yourself to wait in this darkness as long as necessary,
but still go on longing after him whom you love. For if you are
to feel him in this life, it must always be in this cloud, in this
darkness.

> — Anonymous fourteenth-century mystic,
> from *The Cloud of Unknowing*

you
wont
Know love
until you've
lost it.

They had come to nest
in the wet marsh, trumpeting
long into the night
their reunion.
You had come silently
like the day's dew, each footstep
a tiny pool
breaking on a leaf's surface.
For this, I loved you.
Loved you, and the geese
in all their unceasing chatter.

All winter
we clung like marmots
burrowing deep in the bed,
kicking snow in moon's face.
I loved you even more.

Loved you
and the whole frozen earth
in her slumber.

Now it's another spring.
She wakes
and all her dreams, readily bound
are sung and cast.
It can only be
she lost her mind, her heart
during the blizzard.
Why else would she pull you
from my sleeping arms?

But sometimes, when I hear them,
I rise from our bed,
slip between the tall grasses
to the muskeg's edge.
Like us, they are throat-singers
pitching
higher and higher, breathing
all their wild heat,
vibrating
the night, the stars
to such frenzy
and still

I go on loving you. Loving you
while the moon,
laughing her reprisal
sinks me deeper, deeper.

Ayîki-pîsim

APRIL ✦ THE FROG MOON

Soft is the phase, this blaze
of orange moon
in my hands,
naked against the night
I lie and wait

the silken black, you
in this place
where moon pauses, passes
over the wet blue/grey rocks
shifts perfectly

in my palms,
I hold fireflies
drumming
a thousand muskeg songs
where you come
to dip your toes, dreaming

the maple trees to flow,
to flow
their sweet secrets,
my arms hollow reeds
bending
to your frog song.

Sâkipakawi-pîsim

Night by day, day by night
all things awaken
on the white stars of midnight.
Amid the deepest green,
the quaking leaves, spruce boughs
green willow and damp moss
we make our altar
and give our naked selves.

Moon, moon
Nôhkom
in my hands I see his face,
carved from pipestone,
fireweed in his eyes,
his mouth canyon flowers,
pink petals opening and falling
like drops of unsung rain
over my flesh, and moon

moon in my hands
he is hard earth, a high cliff wall
I climb and descend
into secret kivas
leaving corndust and prayers,
burn marks etched by my fingers.

iya, iya
his buds sing to my lips,
Nôhkom
his buds are singing, calling
the horses home.

Nôhkom: *Grandmother*
iya, iya: *exclamation of great pleasure*

≫ Paskâwêhowi-pîsim

JUNE ✦ THE HATCHING MOON

Nothing is as it should be.
Moon at my table
is a black wick smoking.
She chokes me on swamp frogs
snickering
to the first sun.
The ducks mind their eggs,
their eyes loose,
loose as snare wire.

Me, I've kissed
the flicker of lizard's tongue.
Now
I want to pluck out his eyes,
pluck out my own
and cast them, all in wailing grief
to the laughing wind.

Nothing is as it should be.
The lake in me is a dry bed
cracking to the bone.
I ache, ache
all that is new
and green and sacred,
all that is reflective of you.

I ache in my smallest bones
but still you won't come
to defend this love.

I curse you
the moon and lizard.
Don't you hear me cracking
bones like wood?
Don't you hear the lullaby
so sweetly red, it bleeds
from the pale stone
splitting my lips?

Nothing is as it should be.
There is only this waiting
and so many songs.

❧ Paskowi-pîsim

The days go on jagged
beneath the skin,
my sinew-slack drum
more silent than the nights
or moon's echo
pulsing her crippled silver.

Everything comes to stillness
at this hour.

How many nights, now
without you?
The clouds hang on the sky
waiting rainmaker's lulling song.
Me, I have skin and veins
to offer anyone, hungry.
I have at least these,
torn and diluted as they are.

Everything comes to silence
at this hour.

On whose pillow do you lay
your vagrant head?
Whose hands
pulled you from my dreams?

Tonight
I sleep under a duck's shadow
whose naked wings
sew my mouth like a seam

and everything alive, once fluttering
and hopeful
comes to death.

Ohpahôwi-pîsim

AUGUST ✦ THE FLYING-UP MOON

Most unexpected,

you roll into me like a stone
sinking deep in the earth,
settling deeper
than all the moons
having crawled across the sky,
crouched low and silent,
soft-boned and remorseful
as the skinny willows
rattling in the wind.

Now
I cannot name your absence
or its taste,
a strange language
neither bitter nor sweet.

Only you've returned,
a heavy-winged bird
and the bed is a pulse
with the weight of desire,
songs that swim beneath our skin,
lay drunk like fish
in stifling pools.

Though this longing is no secret
you hold it close,
press into me, helpless
against your shame.

Finally you've come!
piko kîkway miyonâkwan.

You sing the summer's end
between my thighs, kiss
the swollen moon
in the curve of my belly,

me, flying-up
like the ducks in the marsh,
you, new-feathered
and weightless,

ushering the dancers to my lips.

piko kîkway miyonâkwan: everything is beautiful

➤ Wâstêpakâwi-pîsim

Our bed of grass has turned brown
and leaves are changing
burnt red
and flecked gold
before breaking from the trees
and kissing the river
in separate hungers.

Last night
you bloomed to my touch,
called the birds together
with only a whisper.
We were driving south
on a stretch of road
so endless and smooth
it flowed like water, disappearing
beneath the wheels.

And, looking at you
peering into the limitless night
my thoughts passed over
your precious mouth
where I'd come to plant
my most sacred seed. Love ...

It will be cold soon, you said
clasping my hand,
cupping it between your thighs
where you are always warm.

And we drove, bound by the silence
and behind us, a thousand miles
wrinkled moon's face.

And weasel and rabbit, I said,
will turn their winter white,
my hand squeezing the last blue
from the sky,
pulling you to a warmer climate.

❧ Pinâskowi-pîsim

OCTOBER ✦ THE MIGRATING MOON

â, apisis ê-wî-âcimoyân …
in the moon
when the birds fly south
and the trees
shake their leaves
Coyote took hostage
the long dreaming night.

On his back
he wore all the stars,
but one
which he'd stolen from Moon
while she was sleeping.

But Moon was clever.
She shut down her eye,
called Kiwêtinohk
to dance patterns
on her bare blanket.

And Coyote went blind,
bumped around
till the stars shook free,
till the world
could hear him howling.

To tell this story
would take about one winter.

â, apisis ê-wî-acimoyân: well, I am going to tell a little bit
Kiwêtinohk: *North*

Ayîkopîwi-pîsim

NOVEMBER ✦ THE FROST MOON

He stole in
during the night,
my cold-blooded beggar
climbing my back,
spooning deep into my spine,
begging up all the warmth
you left,
jealous as the trees
quaking their bare limbs.

But these are your two moles,
simply perfect and round.
And these are your lips,
a city of flesh
where no one would starve.
And this is my mouth,
fat and lazy from nibbling
so many nights.

My poor hungry beggar!
He woke me
frozen
like the dead beneath the snow.
Certainly I would be fooled

if he hadn't left tracks
beneath the window.
Certainly I might fall
for his winter spell
if it weren't for your eyes,
hazel as the heat of June.
If it weren't for your fingers,
all ten of them,
long and straight
that coil in my hair
and led my mouth to fields
where horses graze
and toss their heads, dancing
for apples,
sweet as red love.

Oh, I am in such love!
Each dogwood constitutes ceremony,
each root, each thin bone,
each small body of water
turned to ice, each lake
set to sleeping by Wîhtîkow's kiss.

This morning
his ice-blue fingers
strum my lips
begging one summer song,

and really, I don't mind.

Wîhtîkow: *Cannibal or Ice Being. Wîhtîkow stories are*
   usually told in the winter.

Pawâcakinâsîs-pîsim

DECEMBER ✦ THE FROST EXPLODING MOON

And where did we start?
Was it the summer
of my seven year moulting,
the day I thought
another man's body beautiful?
Or was it the spring
and the night
your eyes passed over my naked feet
and lingered such an infinite time?

Perhaps neither.
Perhaps it was only a day
no different from the ones
haphazardly strung together
like the silver bones
of the wind chime
rubbing the night's cool finger.

And though the day eludes me,
I remember that love
galloped in on the backs of horses,
kicked up dust in my heart,
their drumming hooves
carrying you, the dreamrider,
the four corners of the earth

tied together
in a sacred bundle.

But this is the day
of your hateful absence.
Last night stars fell from the sky,
and moon, with her winter cough
hacked all night.
Now I wonder did we kiss good-bye
and was this the last dream?

Tonight there is no trace.
I've searched every valley,
every canyon, every mountain.
You are gone. The horses are gone
and the earth is cold
with all the things I cannot say.

Now
what name is to be given
to the moon?
Coyote has torn her to shreds,
dances wild from the blood of her
to the cracking of the trees,
the frost and my heart exploding.

🦢 Kisê-pîsim

âpihtâ-piponiwi-pîsim
îy, îy
Sâwanohk
the geese have gone,
beneath their wings
sun sleeps
two frost moons.

Like black bear
I count the days:

pôni-ayamihêwi-kîsikâw
nîso-kîsikâw
nîsto-kîsikâw
nêwo-kîsikâw
nîyano-kîsikâw
nîkotwaso-kîsikâw
ayamihêwi-kîsikâw

gather my medicines
snort and paw
pound and chew
hang them in corners,
above the door, my bed

to work in silence
while I dream

niski-pîsim, your song
of yawning flowers
and honey bees

calling the sun, calling
Pîmatisiwin Pêtamawinân

âpihtâ-piponiwi-pîsim: The Half Winter Moon
îy, îy: Exclamation of great heaviness or sadness
Sâwanohk: South
pôni-ayamihêwi-kîsikâw: Sunday is over/Monday
nîso-kîsikâw: Tuesday, the 2nd day
nîsto-kîsikâw: Wednesday, the 3rd day
nêwo-kîsikâw: Thursday, the 4th day
nîyano-kîsikâw: Friday, the 5th day
nîkotwaso-kîsikâw: Saturday, the 6th day
ayamihêwi-kîsikâw: Sunday, the praying day
niski-pîsim: The Goose Moon (March)
Pîmatisiwin Pêtamawinân: Bring Us Life

🕊 Mikisiwi-pîsim

FEBRUARY ✦ THE EAGLE MOON

Though you've been gone more moons
than the earth has seasons,
yesterday
I survived another year,
folded all my lovers
like old clothes in the hope
someone else might fit them.

All this year
my skin was useless,
my bones, a mere formality
till yesterday
the first eagle graced the sky,
ê-papâmihâcik
and circled with such permission
I let loose the mice
who'd come to nest in my mouth.

Before today I had no place.
To say I belonged
to the bed and the night
was not enough.
To say my only song of you
was coaxed from a book,
that life was sung

from the immortal page
and your limbs were real
as tree roots, and you grew tall
and swelled with fruit
was not how I imagined
your ripening or the day
I would be bound by silence
and our small town
which holds more secrets
than our dreambed,
which in a long ago time
we settled into
when the moon was still young.

No. You are not here,
not in blood and bones.
But you are my blood
and my veins throb knowing you exist.
And you are my borrowed bones
which some day will be earth.

Perhaps then meadowlark
will call out the message,
sing it to his brother
who will pick up the song

and carry it on and on
until the news of our reunion
reaches every rock,
kisses every leaf, strokes
the earth's swollen womb
while she births the seasons.

But there is only today,
a small feeble world
wriggling in her cold, cold blanket.
Yet, she will open her mouth
when eagle lands, open it
singing
and finally, this heart will rest.

ê-papâmihâcik: he flew

Autumn's Oath

for Dean

If never

the leaves change
or fall,
the wind speaks up,
sweeps your name
beneath the door
or spider crawls
bringing my last breath
I will have inhaled you
the colours of spring,
tasted summer
in my lungs.

If never

the snow should come and frost
refuses the skinniest limb
my fingers will have passed
over your flesh
and my lips, red from love
will swell with tranquility
like moon on the lake,
casting up

the soldier-standing trees
upon the bank.

If never

in this season
little winter sparrow
brings you my whole heart
then I shall wait,
heavy with song but warmed
by the very thought
of singing.

And should the leaves change,
fall from the trees
and all the birds
take south my voice,
my tongue will know
your language,
sweet and spiced,
and I will have loved you
to the season's fullest.

LOVE MEDICINE AND ONE SONG

Medicine Lodge

nêwo kâ-tipiskâk, hâw
I dream the poles
long and straight,
Nôcokwesiw's finger pointing
down from the sky
telling me,
nôsisim, kakweyâhok, waniskâ!

nêwo kâ-tipiskâk, hâw
I lift and raise,
place each one
humming circle songs
to line
Thunderbird's nest.

nêwo kâ-tipiskâk, hâw
I dream my skin
a snake's shedding.
I weep and cut,
stitch and paint
moon and stars

until

the womb welcomes me

in the lodge
I lie and wait
heavy with birth,
plump with songs.

She gathers medicine
from the muskeg
and so I shall heal
all that is lost.

nêwo kâ-tipiskâk, hâw: four nights, now
Nôcokwesiw's: Old Woman's
nôsisim, kakweyâhok, waniskâ: Grandson, hurry, wake up

❧ Ceremonies

I heat the stones
between your legs,
my mouth,
the lodge where you come
to sweat.

I fast your lips
commune with spirits,
fly over berry bushes
hungering.

I dance with sun,
float with clouds
your earth smell
deep in my nostrils,
wetting
the tip of my tongue.

I chant with frogs,
sing you to dreams,
bathe you in muskeg,
wrap you in juniper
and sweet-pine.

nîcimos, for you
I drink blessed water,

chew the bitter roots
so the medicine is sweet,
the love, sacred.

nîcimos: *sweetheart or lover*

ꙮ Old Time Medicine, I

She said,

take a ribbon
the colour of sky

and white, pure
must be pure

the ribbons and smudge them
through sweet willow fungus

smoke in spring
when the moon is fullest

thinking the purest
of pure thoughts

calling the stars
down and

above your lover's bed
they will fall and swirl

and on this night
your fingers shall sing

their medicine song
as if his own

heartbeat was drummed
but no, not

till his waking
will there be a hint

how medicine came
and went and left

a longing so pure and blue
he will know

the clouds in your eyes,
lake of your mouth

and drink your presence,
float with your words

if thoughtfully, most purely
you pin them

under clothes, wrap wrists
ankles

taking care, great care
to touch him

softly in passing

❧ Whispers and Thoughts

The old people say
it's all medicine.
Even this whisper cast up
from heart's mould,
my one hundred
white butterflies
as real as kisses
blown one hundred times,
beating all two hundred wings
and landing
the blushed flower of your mouth
but once.

tapwê Nitotemak,
these are the days
I want to be wide open,
sing loud
the medicine of me,
unpack the thoughts
I've stored all winter long,
hang my robin's eyes
the whole bright day
while he flits in and out,
me, full-bellied and him,
charming as the sun.

tapwê Nitotemak: *for sure, my relations*

❧ Old Time Medicine, 2

aya kayâs,
the promise might be
horses, blankets
even your first born.

aya kayâs,
things were done thoughtfully
like a word, pêyahtihk
said with great care
so as not to offend
the listener.

êkwa kayâs,
all would have been
hush, hush.
Maybe you sneak
in the night
to Old Man's lodge,
lay out your love-sick heart
for him to poke and prod.
Maybe smoke his pipe,
not speaking for hours
till he sums up
the nature of your sickness,
sums the grandfathers
to tickle his ears.

êkwa êkosi kayâs
ê-kiskêyihtaman
listening and watching.
Old Man might cut figures
from birch bark,
sing a little
and dab his medicine
first to one heart, crying,
êy! êy! kimisken.
Then to the other, teasing,
wahwâ, kani tapwê ôma!

aya kayâs: *a long time ago*
pêyahtihk: *to give something great thought, to walk softly*
êkwa kayâs: *and a long time ago*
êkwa êkosi kayâs e-kiskêyihtaman: *and years ago that is*
      how you learned
êy! êy! kimisken: *Hey! Hey! You found it*
wahwâ, kani tapwê ôma: *Oh goodness, it is true*

Night Train

Tonight
I am in dual love.
Praise all! Praise
the slippery eye, praise to
the transient night, my weary travellers.

Praise
to this narcotic hour
fleeing so quickly
like sparks
whistling down the track.

Tonight
I am in dual love, no
I am in love double: $1 + 1 = 3$
counting him, her and me, and

if you added
his perfect lips, her perfect arms
multiplied my heart, counted
all the sensations
I subtract and divide and
put together like so many railcars
my skeleton would stretch
a love song from here
to eternity.

And praise
to all this motion, the eyes trailing
their week-long bags,
praise to the bed
and the loveliness we'll make.

Tonight
I am in dual love. Praise!

She will carry his song
sing it for days,
and he, my shadowed engineer
will ride straight through,
whistle me
a slow beat against the night.

I Brought Her Horses

I brought her horses:
pinto, appaloosa, mustang —

I brought her
bellowing nostrils, braided tails
from the sacred valley
where earth is sky —

I brought her
wind runners, the quickest of all
tethered them

outside her lodge
I offered my flute,
twilight and cricket songs
I hummed
down the smoke-hole,
nestled
beneath her robe, my thighs
sinew and muscle, aching
from the long ride home.

tapwêsa, my love
I brought her horses:
pinto, appaloosa, mustang —

of these I gave the finest,
her father's eyes
low with the accepting.

tapwêsa: *this is true*

🍃 The Birthday Gift

How much she loves me
loving you
is more than all the stars
or nights I've spent
crouched over words, placing them
like some infinite puzzle,
fitting all the pieces
of heart, flesh and bone together,
collecting them piecemeal,
my treasured loves
older than rare china
found on a perfect sunday.

Now
it's 4:20 a.m. and the dawning
of your quarter century,
my sleeping angel Gabriel
with blackwings
spread out on the pillow, blackwings
the colour of a pure northern night
when it comes down.

But it's merely metaphor,
this sacred hour. The hour
Sky Grandfather
wipes the stars from his eyes,

stretches
between moon and sun, releases
the birds
to sit on the day's lips.

And we, my love and I
sneak to your doorway
like Christmas children –
she in my robe, dreamy
as the sky's breaking, and me
determined as yesterday
to fill your ears
with one sweet song.

⤜ Sâkihtowin-Maskihkiy ✦ Love Medicine

Pêyahtihk, the old people would say,
their eyes
heavy with thunder, each word
a sermon taking flight
on câhcâhkayowak's wings.

Still, I dream him
four sacred moon faces:
Pipon, Miyoskamin, Nîpin, Takwâkin.

I dream
the delicacy of his lips,
taste damp earth
on the tip of his tongue.
I dream flute songs,
chase the echo
in my heart's canyon.

Helpless against this love
I contemplate trading
sunsets and stars
for even the faintest
hint of medicine.

Pêyahtihk, the old people would say,
and three words he whispers

so wild horses
fill my ears, my heart
runs reckless,
so I forget the sermon
these raven shadows
hovering.

Pêyahtihk: *to give something great thought, to walk softly*
câhcâhkayowak's: *blackbird's*
Pipon: *Winter*
Miyoskamin: *Spring*
Nîpin: *Summer*
Takwâkin: *Fall*

❧ Pêyak-Nikamowin ✦ One Song

At the break of dawn
the spirits I call
to the west, the south,
the north, the east
I am looking
like them I am looking
calling to my love.

âstam ôta nîcimos
ôtantâyan, ôtantâyan
hey-ya-ho-ho
hey-ya-ho-ho
hey-ya-ho-ho
hey-ya-ho-ho

In this dream
he is across the river
standing upon the bank
just over there
my sweetheart.

kâya mâto nîcimos
kinîtôhtan, kinîtôhtan
hey-ya-ho-ho
hey-ya-ho-ho
hey-ya-ho-ho
hey-ya-ho-ho

I am going to cross
to where he is
cross that river
for my love
but he is gone
and the reeds are weeping.

kakwêyahok nîcimos
ninêstosin, ninêstosin
hey-ya-ho-ho
hey-ya-ho-ho
hey-ya-ho-ho
hey-ya-ho-ho

Now all I have are
rainberries and tears to give
as I sit here
watching where he stood.

pekîwêyan nîcimos
nî-mâtoyân, nî-mâtoyân
hey-ya-ho-ho
hey-ya-ho-ho
hey-ya-ho-ho
hey-ya-ho-ho

âstam ôta nîcimos
ôtantâyan, ôtantâyan:
come here my sweetheart
I am here, I am here

kâya mâto nîcimos
kinîtôhtan, kinîtôhtan:
don't cry my sweetheart
I hear you, I hear you

kakwêyahok nîcimos
ninêstosin, ninêstosin:
hurry my sweetheart
I am tired, I am tired

pekîwêyan nîcimos
nî-mâtoyân, nî-mâtoyân:
come home my sweetheart
I am crying, I am crying

Gregory Scofield is a Mixed-blood poet, storyteller, activist and community worker of Cree, Scottish, English and French ancestry. He was born in Paskowi-pîsim – the Moulting Moon – in British Columbia, and raised in northen Saskatchewan, northern Manitoba and the Yukon.

His first book, *The Gathering: Stones for the Medicine Wheel* (Polestar), is a biographical collection of poetry reflecting his journey toward spiritual growth. It was awarded the Dorothy Livesay Poetry Prize. Scofield won the Canadian Author's Association Most Promising Young Writer Award for his second book, *Native Canadiana: Songs From The Urban Rez* (Polestar). His poems have appeared in anthologies such as *Breathing Fire: Canada's New Poets* (Harbour), *Voices of the First Nations, Windhorse Reader: Choice Poems of '93, ARC* and *An Anthology of Canadian Native Literature in English* (Oxford).

Gregory lives in Maple Ridge, B.C. with his partner Kim, their dog Âski and cat Pjat. He devotes his time to writing and travelling.